Table of Contents

Wild Weather

Imagine you just finished setting up for a party in the park with your friends. It's a warm, sunny day. You have a huge water balloon fight planned. There is a rock-climbing wall to race up and delicious treats to share. You can't wait for the fun to begin!

Suddenly, the sky grows dark. The wind picks up, and your hair begins to blow in every direction. There's a bright flash of lightning in the sky. It's followed closely by a loud crash of thunder. Raindrops start falling from the sky. Minutes later, everything is drenched. The **weather** forecast did not mention a storm. But here it is. Is the party over? Maybe not—but it is definitely about to get wet!

Extreme Weather

Weather

Torrey Maloof

Consultant

Catherine Hollinger, CID, CLIA
EPA WaterSense Partner
Environmental Consultant

Image Credits: Cover & p.1 Tom Wang/Alamy, p.21
Andrew McConnell/Alamy; p.22 Derek Croucher/
Alamy; p.7 (top) Ilene MacDonald/Alamy; p.27
Jochen Tack/Alamy; p.19 Nigel Cattlin/Alamy; p.17
RGB Ventures/SuperStock/Alamy; pp.20, 32 Ted
Foxx/Alamy; p.26 US Marines Photo/Alamy; pp.7,
24 (illustrations) Tim Bradley; p.15 (right bottom)
Flickr/Getty Images; p.15 (left bottom) Simon Tonge/
Getty Images pp.5, 7 (right) 8, 10, 15, 30 iStock;
p.24 The Library of Congress, LC-USZ62-043668;
p.13 (top) NASA; pp.12–13 DanitaDelimont.com/
Newscom (background); p.9 MCT/Newscom; p.31
Polaris/Newscom; p.15 (top) Reuters/Newscom;
p.23 ANT Photo Library/Science Source; p.22 El
Niño Southern Oscillation (ENSO)/NOAA; p.16 Eye
of Science/Science Source; p.6 Frans Lanting/MINT
Images/Science Source; p.9 Gary Hincks/Science
Source; p.11 Julie Dermansky/Science Source (4th
down); pp.2–3 Roger Hill/Science Source; pp.28–29
(illustrations) J.J. Rudisill; pp.10, 15 (background)
Wikipedia; all other images from Shutterstock.

Library of Congress Cataloging-in-Publication Data

Maloof, Torrey, author.
 Extreme weather / Torrey Maloof.
  pages cm
 Summary: "Twirling tornadoes, horrific hurricanes,
deadly dust storms, and blowing blizzards. Depending
where you live, you may have experienced one of these
frightening storms. Although being caught in extreme
weather can be dangerous, being prepared can save
your life!"—Provided by publisher.
 Audience: K to grade 3.
 Includes index.
 ISBN 978-1-4807-4647-3 (pbk.)
 ISBN 1-4807-4647-9 (pbk.)
 ISBN 978-1-4807-5091-3 (ebook)
 1. Climatic extremes—Juvenile literature.
 2. Storms—Juvenile literature.
 3. Weather—Juvenile literature. I. Title.
 QC981.8.C53M35 2015
 551.55—dc23
                          2014034277

Teacher Created Materials

5301 Oceanus Drive
Huntington Beach, CA 92649-1030
http://www.tcmpub.com
ISBN 978-1-4807-4647-3

Lightning strikes somewhere on Earth every second!

Meteorologists are people who study the weather. You may see them on your local news. They use tools such as radar and satellites to help them. Sometimes, they can **predict** the weather. But other times, it is hard to know what the weather will be.

Weather is the state of the air at a certain place and time. Most weather is mild. It may be sunny and warm. Or there may be light snow. But sometimes, the weather can be downright wild! A tornado or a hurricane may blow through a city. A dust storm may consume a town. Blizzards may cover entire cities in snow. This wild weather is dangerous. It is important to study this weather so we can be prepared.

People walk through a dust storm.

ENHANCED SATELLITE

3:35 PM

What's the Weather?

March	🌡️	🌧️	☁️	🎏
1. Mild with light rain 10:00 AM	12°C	💧	◑	
2. rained most of the day 10:15 AM	11°C	💧💧	●	←
3. partly sunny 10:20 AM	9°C		◔	↖
4. cool and windy 10:05 AM	8°C		○	↖
5. clear with a rainbow 10:25 AM	10°C	💧	◑	→
6. mild, drizzle 9:50 AM	10°C	💧	◕	→
7. WEEKLY SUMMARY AND AVERAGES	10°C		◑	

7

Terrifying Tornadoes

Have you ever seen *The Wizard of Oz*? It's the movie with Dorothy and her ruby red slippers. And her little dog, too! In the movie, Dorothy gets swept up in a tornado. It takes her to an enchanted land. While this may make for a great movie, in real life, tornadoes don't whisk you away to magical places. In fact, you should always seek shelter from tornadoes. They are dangerous!

Tornadoes are sometimes called twisters. Can you guess why?

Staying Safe

The safest place to be during a tornado is underground. A basement or a storm shelter will keep you safe. If you cannot get underground, go to the center of a building. And stay away from windows!

Tornadoes are **funnels** of powerful wind. They occur during thunderstorms. The wind moves around a central point. The wind can reach speeds of over 400 kilometers per hour (250 miles per hour). Tornadoes act like giant vacuums. They suck up everything in their path. They can pick up cars and toss them like toys. Tornadoes tear houses apart. They destroy buildings. They are one of the most violent forces in nature.

Tetsuya Fujita (tet-SOO-yah foo-JEE-tuh) was a tornado expert. The Fujita scale is named after him. Scientists around the world use this scale to rate tornadoes. It is based on the damage a tornado can cause. It also measures wind speed. The low end of the scale is EF0. This is a small tornado. The worst tornado is an EF5.

On May 22, 2011, an EF5 tornado hit Joplin, Missouri (mi-ZOOR-ee). It was a Sunday afternoon. The weather was humid and hot. No one in Joplin knew that a powerful tornado was about to tear through their town. The massive twister flattened homes. It ripped up streets. It sent debris flying. At one point, the tornado was almost a mile wide! Over 100 people lost their lives. Many more were injured. There was over $2.1 billion in damage.

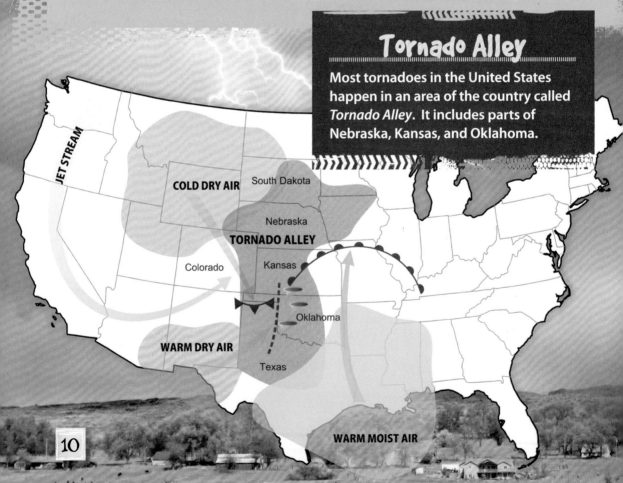

Tornado Alley

Most tornadoes in the United States happen in an area of the country called *Tornado Alley*. It includes parts of Nebraska, Kansas, and Oklahoma.

JET STREAM

COLD DRY AIR

South Dakota

Nebraska

TORNADO ALLEY

Colorado

Kansas

Oklahoma

WARM DRY AIR

Texas

WARM MOIST AIR

The Fujita Scale

Scale	Wind Speed (kmh)	Wind Speed (mph)	Example
EF0	105–137	65–85	
EF1	138–178	86–110	
EF2	179–218	111–135	
EF3	219–266	136–165	
EF4	267–322	166–200	
EF5	greater than 322	greater than 200	

Horrendous Hurricanes

When hurricanes are out at sea, they cause little damage. But when these storms hit land, they are very destructive. Hurricanes bring heavy rain and strong winds.

Hurricanes begin as tropical storms. But when a storm reaches 119 kmh (74 mph), it changes. It begins to pick up warm water from the ocean. The water is in the form of **vapor**. This vapor **condenses** to form clouds. The clouds form a spiral. An "eye" can be seen in the center of the hurricane. In the eye, the weather is calm. Outside the eye, the weather is chaotic (key-OT-ik).

Staying Dry

If you live in an area with hurricanes, you can stay dry—and safe—by following these steps:

- Listen to the radio or watch TV for warnings.
- Stay inside, close windows and doors, bring in pets, and secure any objects left outside.
- Talk with your family about where you can go during a hurricane.

EVACUATION ROUTE

On October 29, 2012, the coasts of New York and New Jersey began to flood. Huge waves pounded the shoreline. Water poured into homes. Subways filled with water. That night, a hurricane came ashore. It was Hurricane Sandy. When the sun rose the next day, people could not believe what they saw. There were billions of dollars in damage. Millions of people were without power. Thousands of people had lost their homes. And many people had lost their lives.

Hurricane Sandy was one of the biggest storms in history. It affected more than 12 states. It also hit the Caribbean and Canada. Strong winds and **storm surges** caused the most damage. New York and New Jersey were hit the hardest. But the people in these states worked together. They fixed their homes. They rebuilt their businesses. They helped one another.

2004
Hurricane Ivan

2005
Hurricane Katrina

2012
Hurricane Sandy

The Naming System

The World Meteorological Organization has lists of names that are assigned to hurricanes. When a hurricane causes a lot of damage, the name is retired from the list.

2008
Hurricane Ike

2005
Hurricane Wilma

Disastrous Dust Storms

Do your parents ever ask you to help clean? Have you ever wiped dust off a shelf or a television screen? Dust **accumulates** quickly. It floats in the air before it settles on the ground or on an object. And if you do not wipe it away, it will soon cover everything in your home! But what is dust?

Dust is made of many different things. Thread or lint from your clothing becomes dust. Pollen and pieces of plants form dust. Bits of rubber from car tires and flakes of dead skin dissolve into dust. Dust seems harmless enough until large quantities build up in our atmosphere.

dust magnified under a powerful microscope

Ah-Choo!

Sometimes, dust gets in your nose. If this happens, grab a tissue quickly! You are about to sneeze. Sneezing is your body's way of getting rid of dust.

A woman in England once sneezed 978 days in a row!

Dust devils are like mini tornadoes.
They form when wind, dust,
and debris combine.

Dust in your house isn't very dangerous. It may make your eyes red, or it may cause you to sneeze once in a while. But if you keep your house clean, you will be just fine. Dust *outside* your house is another story.

When strong winds combine with dry conditions, dust storms appear. Fierce winds kick up large amounts of dust. The dust travels up into the atmosphere and is pushed by the wind. This creates large dust clouds. These clouds can cover entire cities and rise more than 10 kilometers (6 miles) into the air! They make it nearly impossible to see. They also carry toxic, or harmful, **particles**. This makes it very hard to breathe. It can also make people ill.

Dangerous Droughts

A drought is a long period of dryness. This means there is very little or no rain. Droughts are one cause of dust storms.

Dust storms often happen in deserts. Deserts are dry and have very few plants. Plants help keep soil in place. Without plants to anchor dry soil, winds can pick up dust and create dust storms. This happened in Arizona in July of 2012.

A dust storm that was 160 km (100 mi) wide swept across the Arizona desert. The sun was completely blocked out. Airplanes could not land. Drivers could not see the road in front of them. The dust storm was so powerful that it caused the power to go out. People's homes and businesses filled with dust. Swimming pools were turned into mud baths. The storm lasted for over 20 minutes. Luckily, no one was hurt, but everyone had a big mess to clean up!

dust storm in Yuma, Arizona

Staying out of the Storm

Dust storms can occur quickly. It is best to stay inside. But if you are caught outside in a storm, follow these tips:

- Wear a cloth over your nose and mouth.
- Wear eyeglasses to protect your eyes.
- Apply petroleum jelly to the inside of your nose to keep it from drying out.
- Move to higher ground.
- Try to find shelter!

dust storm in Africa

Brrr... Blizzards!

Snowball fights are fun. So is building a snowman. But too much snow can be a bad thing. Blizzards bring a lot of snow. And they bring it fast! A blizzard is a fierce winter storm with strong winds and very cold temperatures.

Blizzards happen when powerful winds called **jet streams** hit warmer air. The jet stream is pushed down while the warm air is pushed up. This creates snow and ice. Strong winds blow the snow. Those caught in a blizzard find it difficult to see. And these fierce winds make the air feel even colder than it really is. This is called the *wind-chill factor*. If it is -1° Celsius (30° Fahrenheit) outside, it can feel like it is -20°C (-4°F) in cold, strong winds.

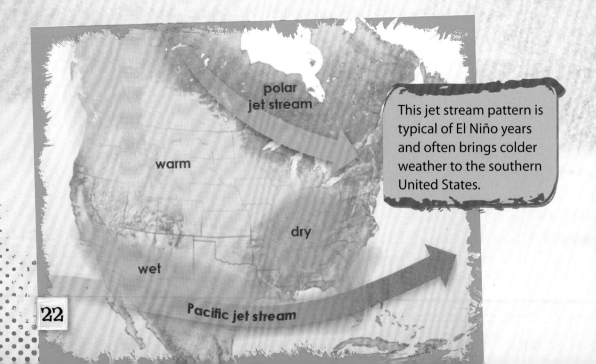

polar jet stream

warm

dry

wet

Pacific jet stream

This jet stream pattern is typical of El Niño years and often brings colder weather to the southern United States.

Frostbite

Frostbite happens when not enough blood flows to the hands, feet, and ears. Skin tissue is destroyed. Sometimes, toes and fingers need to be amputated, or cut off, to cure the frostbite. Wearing layers can help prevent frostbite.

A blackout occurs when power is lost and all the lights go off. A whiteout happens during a blizzard when all you can see is snow.

One of the worst blizzards in history occurred over 100 years ago. Back then, predicting the weather was even harder than it is today. There were no satellites, and scientists didn't use radar yet. No one knew when a storm was coming. It had been an unusually warm day in March on the East Coast of the United States. But then, the warm jet-stream air from the Gulf of Mexico mixed with cold arctic air from Canada. The blizzard had begun!

The Great Blizzard of 1888 affected cities from Washington, DC, to Maine. It took only a few hours before there was about 140 centimeters (55 inches) of snow on the ground. Wind gusts blew over 137 kmh (85 mph). The blizzard took the lives of many people. Today, meteorologists can warn people about approaching blizzards.

Make Your Own Pocket Hand Warmers

All you need is natural felt, a needle, thread, and some rice! Then, 30 seconds in the microwave will finish your hand warmers.

Lesson Learned

Many people were trapped on trains in New York City during the Great Blizzard of 1888. After the blizzard, the city decided to move its trains underground. This subway system is used in New York City today.

Be Prepared!

Weather can take many forms. On a sunny day, the sky can be filled with fluffy clouds. But during a storm, the water in the air can quickly turn into rain, hail, or a flurry of snowflakes. A cool breeze can feel refreshing on a hot day. But wind can become wild and dangerous in a hurricane or a tornado.

People board a plane to escape a hurricane in the Philippines.

The weather is constantly changing. It's always a good idea to check the weather forecast. This way you can be prepared. When the weather is extreme, you must make smart choices. If a tornado is coming, seek shelter. Try to get underground as fast as possible. If a hurricane is coming, you may need to **evacuate**. This means you leave your home. Go somewhere safe where the storm will not affect you. If a dust storm is coming, it is best to stay inside, away from the dust. And if a blizzard is coming, stay indoors where it is warm.

If you are prepared, you can handle any weather Mother Nature may throw your way!

Think Like a Scientist

How does a tornado move? Experiment and find out!

What to Get

⊃ 2 large soda bottles

⊃ duct tape

⊃ food coloring

⊃ glitter (optional)

⊃ scissors

⊃ water

What to Do

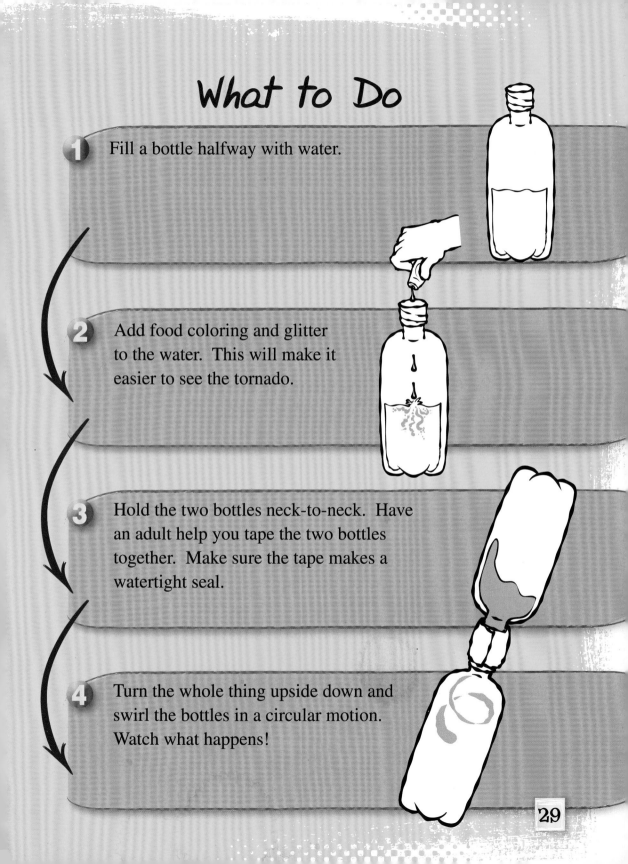

1 Fill a bottle halfway with water.

2 Add food coloring and glitter to the water. This will make it easier to see the tornado.

3 Hold the two bottles neck-to-neck. Have an adult help you tape the two bottles together. Make sure the tape makes a watertight seal.

4 Turn the whole thing upside down and swirl the bottles in a circular motion. Watch what happens!

Glossary

accumulates—gathers or piles up little by little

condenses—changes from a gas into a liquid

evacuate—to leave a dangerous place

funnels—things shaped like hollow cones

jet streams—strong currents of fast winds high above Earth's surface

meteorologists—people who study the atmosphere, weather, and weather forecasting

particles—very small pieces of something

predict—to say that something will or might happen in the future

storm surges—unusual rises in the level of the sea along a coast

vapor—a substance in the form of a gas

weather—the state of the air and atmosphere at a particular time and place

Index

Your Turn!

Wacky Weather

Have you seen a lightning storm? Maybe you've been caught in a blizzard. What extreme weather have you experienced? Write a journal entry about a time you saw some wacky weather. Draw a picture to go with your journal entry.